Rosemary for Remembrance

A Personal Tribute to Those Who Served in the World Wars

Anne P Stewart

Rosemary for Remembrance

ISBN: 978-1-9161333-1-0

Copy edited by Ian Large

Cover by Jag Lall based on an original design by Tom Maddocks

This book is produced by Anne Stewart Publishing in conjunction with WRITERSWORLD, and is produced entirely in the UK. It is available to order from most bookshops in the United Kingdom, and is also globally available via UK based Internet book retailers.

WRITERSWORLD
2 Bear Close Flats, Bear Close, Woodstock
Oxfordshire, OX20 1JX, England

☎ 01993 812500
☎ +44 1993 812500

www.writersworld.co.uk

The text pages of this book are produced via an independent certification process that ensures the trees from which the paper is produced come from well managed sources that exclude the risk of using illegally logged timber while leaving options to use post-consumer recycled paper as well.

For my Grandchildren

Emma, Jack, Lucy, Tom and William

With my love and pride of your achievements to date.

Grandma Anne

CONTENTS

Green for the fields in which they died,

Red for the poppies we wear with pride

and a sprig of Rosemary lest we forget all they did.

INTRODUCTION

This small collection of poems is my tribute to the enormous sacrifice made by so many young men in two world wars.

It is also an acknowledgement of a long-lasting friendship with Lucienne Lerch and her family from the village of Marmoutier in Alsace, a friendship forged through the opportunity of a school exchange, which our fathers encouraged, having each served in both world wars. Sadly our fathers were never to meet but they shared the hope that a better understanding between nations would lessen the risk of further world wars.

There have been many moments when I have wished that I had asked my father more about his war experience, especially in WW1. However, from books I have read, I do know that many men, on returning home, were advised not to speak about their experiences. I have also recognised that there is a comradeship between those who served in wars that is so strong that those of us who were not involved cannot even begin to penetrate its depth.

William Shakespeare describes this comradeship so vividly in his play, *Henry V*, when Henry describes those who will fight with him on Crispin's Day as, *"We few, we happy few, we band of brothers. For he today that sheds his blood with me, shall be my brother."*

Looking back over my life there is nothing which might have

alerted me to think that I would be writing poetry in later life. However, I do recall my father saying that his father wrote all his letters to my grandmother in blank verse. On another occasion I found a book on my maternal grandmother's shelves called *Poems* by Tom the Postman. Family history research by my cousin Peter Henriksen has shown that this is a close relative of our mother's and a recognised published poet about whom we hope to gain more information.

Anne and Lucienne, c.1950

When Lucienne and I first met we were barely able to speak each other's language and were coping with the unsettling teen years. However, we managed to maintain the friendship and today count our blessings when we have occasion to meet and look back over the years of friendship. It would therefore have been remiss of me not to have mentioned it, because visits to France have taught me so much about the conflicts and allowed me to visit many of the battlefields where it all took place.

Alsace was German territory from 1870 to 1918, when it became French, so Lucienne's father, Lucien, fought in the German Army in WW1, serving mostly on the Russian front.

Illustration by Pascal Klein

However, when Alsace was annexed by Germany in 1940, resistance against the German occupation was apparently very strong and it is now known that Lucien joined a resistance group and is mentioned as a leader in a book written after the war ended. He never mentioned his work to the family, perhaps because of the dangers and possible reprisals, and the family have no personal mementos.

I am dedicating this anthology to my grandchildren, in the hope that they will take every opportunity to travel widely and perhaps forge friendships with some they meet on their travels. Most importantly I want them to have pride and awareness of the history of our country, and an understanding of why their great grandfather Henry Walton and grandfather Michael Aldworth fought so hard with others for freedom from oppression by those who sought to dominate.

At the same time I sincerely hope that Lucienne, and the many French friends I have gained, know how much I appreciate the friendship we share and the part they and many others, sadly no longer with us, have all played in welcoming me and willingly shared their memories and hospitality.

Lucien Lerch
28/7/1895 – 1958

ACKNOWLEDGEMENTS

I am grateful for the help and encouragement offered by so many people when compiling this anthology.

Ian large and Jag Lall from WRITERSWORLD, whose endless patience and advice made this journey so enjoyable, and to Graham Cook who initially thought my work worthy of publishing.

Martyn Lockwood, our lay-reader at church who encouraged me to read my poems at Remembrance services.

Graeme Cooper, our battlefield guide, whose expertise as a soldier and of the many battlefields we toured, taught me so much.

My family who, although astonished to find me contemplating publishing, nevertheless stood by my decision and offered help in so many ways.

My grandson Tom, whose design for the cover was accepted by WRITERSWORLD, with only minor alterations.

Our French friend Pascal Klein, who offered the design to illustrate the friendship Lucienne and I continue to enjoy.

Colleen Jorgensen, an American artist who painted the sprig of rosemary for the front cover.

Thank you to Alamy.com for the photos of Passchendaele and Tyne Cot.

I have sought permission for use of *Weariness* from Daniel Foucart, but as yet have not received any response. I hope that he does not object to its inclusion.

My daughter-in-law Jane for her photographs of fields of poppies and Marie-France Lerch for her photograph of Lucien Lerch.

Last but by no means least, my husband Jack, who encouraged me through the many hours when I doubted my ability when the words failed to flow as I wished.

To you all and the many friends both in the UK and France who never doubted that one day the book would be finished, I offer you my sincere thanks and hope the long wait was worthwhile.

Anne P Stewart.

IN MEMORY OF MY FATHER

I knew you nearly forty years, a lifetime so it seems.
You watched my early childhood and had so many dreams.
You had to leave when I was small to fight to guard our
shores,
I was so young, there wasn't time to know you well at all.
God sent you back to us again to take your place once more,
but now it felt a lifetime since you went out the door.
To me you were a stranger and oh how hard it seemed,
to re-establish friendship of which we'd only dreamed.
We tried so hard both you and I to get to know each other,
but you had been away so long at war with soldier brother.

Then age crept up upon you as years went rolling by
and with it came the illness which meant you were to die.
Of course we did not mention it, we were too worldly wise,
but when I looked upon your face, I read it in your eyes.
No longer sure of everything, you showed your fear and
stress.
You were so much frustrated and full of bitterness.
And so we changed our roles in life, the young one you
became,
while I became the parent to ease away your pain.
But once more we established a closeness very true,
which this time will remain intact, when I return to you.

Background to *IN MEMORY OF MY FATHER*

It is difficult for later generations to understand the impact and changes on the social structure after a world war. The knowledge that we lost a whole generation of young men in WW1, leaving many women without the chance of marrying and those widowed in dire straits financially, is difficult to appreciate unless personally experienced.

Women in both world wars took on responsibilities never imagined before and men returning as heroes, many disfigured or disabled, were frustrated and angry to find themselves without a job. The impact on children being introduced to strange men as their fathers also had its effect and many families struggled to find a new starting point.

My father was caught up in the mobilisation in the very early days of WW2, having enlisted in the Territorials after recovering from his wounds from WW1. I was barely five years old but had several memories of him. He was later sent to Burma to take charge of a Gurkha regiment so we saw little of him until the end of hostilities.

I was eleven when he returned but during his absence my mother, like so many other women, had to take on many responsibilities plus my upbringing single-handedly. She was one of the first to volunteer to assemble gas masks and later served lunches in one of what were called British Restaurants where for a small sum you could get a two-course lunch. She also helped at a local hospital distributing library books round the wards.

My father returned to a job in the Town Hall at Newcastle-upon-Tyne as a committee clerk, but resented the loss of status, having been used to command. So my parents too must have experienced difficulties as my father, like so many other returning men, expected everything to be exactly the same as before.

My mother and I had created a life for ourselves to cope as best we could and it was difficult, I have to admit, to accept my father's Victorian attitude, which included me being seen but not heard. I soon realised that unless my thoughts and feelings agreed with those of my father they were likely to be brushed aside, so it was easier to keep my thoughts to myself. For a long time it did affect my confidence. I also recognised a change in my mother as she was now expected to run the home and leave other responsibilities to my father.

However, I recognise now that my father saw this as looking after us and would not have wanted to be regarded as being unable to provide for his family. Most certainly we were loved in his own way.

The older I became I began to appreciate more the difficulties my parents must have experienced and I cannot deny it was a relief to start my independent life as a trainee nurse at the age of eighteen. However, age brings wisdom of many kinds and when my father was found to have throat cancer, I was better prepared and more self-assured and understanding of his feelings. He showed his resentment and frustration in so many ways. No longer in complete control of his life, having to rely on others for his care, cannot have been easy having given so much, like so many others, to the service of his country.

On the rare occasions that my father spoke of his war experience, unless questioned directly, he always referred to his regiment as The Royal Artillery.

It was therefore a great surprise to discover on the rim of his WW1 medals his service number 19678 and the words Bedfordshire Regiment; something he never mentioned as far as I am aware. This prompted a visit to the regimental museum at Luton and being recommended to contact Steven Fuller who was writing the regimental history.

Henry Walton's WW1 & WW2 medals.

Steven was kind enough to guide me through the beginning of a search for more details and he was able to tell me that father enlisted in 1915 and that after training he landed in France on October 27th 1915 as part of replacements for regimental losses at the Battle of Loos. Sadly, the battalion history seems to have been lost at this point. Further research through Forces World War records provided a few more details. However, it has to be acknowledged that a lot of war records were destroyed or damaged during the Blitz so I was lucky to have found some reference to him.

It is interesting how much information can be recognised from the insignia on uniforms and hat badges by those who have studied the war in depth. Graeme Cooper, our battlefield guide and a retired senior officer from The Green Howards regiment, immediately spotted the insignia on father's jacket sleeve that indicated that he had been a 'sharp shooter' or sniper and would have received extra pay.

Discoveries of this kind plus the oak leaf on his ribbons indicating he was mentioned in despatches, certainly added to my frustrations of having no details. My husband did ask him on one occasion what the oak leaf was awarded for but received the answer, "Oh they came up with the rations."

Whether this was a genuine reluctance to talk about his experiences, or because of the warning those returning from WW1 were given, not to mention all they had witnessed when they got home, I shall never know. However, having learned and seen for myself the psychological effects of trauma of this kind that some people experience, I am amazed that we did not learn of more suicides and mental withdrawal by troops once they were home, especially as they found a different homeland and attitude to the one they had known before they left to serve their country.

It was early in 1918 before father was seriously wounded. At first he was sent to a dressing station because of a wound to his wrist. However, they redirected him to a field hospital for further care, but had no transport, just directions, so he had to walk. During this journey he was found by the Military Police, who thought he was a deserter until he collapsed, having been also wounded through a lung. They transported him to the field hospital but staff there recognised he needed more specialised treatment and he was placed on a barge which was on the point of leaving for a port, where once again luck was with him as a troop ship was about to sail for the UK where he was treated at a hospital in Great Ormond Street.

One day he was asked to name his favourite meal, which he recognised as being a question they were asked if expected to die. He said blackberry and apple pie, knowing that it was not the season for blackberries. Sepsis must have developed because they wanted to remove his arm but he refused to allow that and, thankfully, whatever treatment followed, the arm was saved.

His war was over at that point and he remained under treatment for a very long time and was officially demobbed in 1919. One well remembered occasion he spoke of to my husband, was being taken with other walking wounded to the first post-war Derby, where they met Lord Derby who marked their race cards.

The scarring on his chest was always a talking point with GPs and radiologists, because of the extensive criss--crossing of the area where it was stitched. One could have easily played noughts and crosses on the pattern.

Many years later, after he died from throat cancer, I was asked permission for a post mortem. As a nurse I knew the value of these but recognised that the request was more a desire to see the inside of his chest where he was wounded and I refused permission because I felt he had been mutilated enough. To my horror I later realised from the death certificate that they overrode my request

In spite of all that he had gone through in WW1, he later joined the Territorials and as soon as WW2 started, he was off to war again, now as a Second Lieutenant, and managed to survive that intact in body but mentally exhausted and the victim of several attacks of malaria.

He served in Burma where he was in charge of a Gurkha regiment who gave him some beautiful pieces of engraved silver, which sadly were stolen from me during a burglary. How I wished I had thought to record the words and name of the regiment engraved on the pieces, but it never entered my head that I would be a victim of theft.

My father was what I believe you would call a born soldier. Two well remembered moments come to mind. One when I took his photographs in uniform to a Family History Fair and one of the gentlemen examining photographs took one look at father in WW1 and with a shake of his head said, "He was but a bairn", and the other was when he vowed at the end of WW2 that he would never take orders from anybody again.

We believe that it was possibly during his time with the Territorials that he was placed in the Royal Artillery and became a gunner. Why he never mentioned his WW1 placement in the Bedfordshire Regiment we shall never know. It is a very proud regiment whose history deserves wide recognition. Despite its activities down the years, I have always had to check books to find references to it in spite of having played an important part in many important battles. This is why I recommend anybody interested in regimental histories to read Steven Fullers *History of the Bedfordshire Regiment*, published by Fighting High Ltd.

Private Harry Walton 17/06/1897 – 25/08/1973

Bedfordshire Regiment 19678, Feb 1915

A SACRED PLACE

Above my head a skylark sings,
hovering on fragile wings.
A relative of those long past,
silenced by the thunderous blast.
While underneath men writhed in pain,
as shells pierced flesh to wound and maim.
Calling to God with piteous cries,
as vision was lost from precious eyes.

Blessed bird let voice be heard,
above these golden fields of wheat.
Where blood red poppies raise their head,
a symbol now of those long dead,
who trod these fields and shed their blood,
in craters filled with putrid mud.

Let homage be paid above this land,
where golden wheat and poppies stand.
For underneath these nurtured fields,
from which emerge past battles needs,
lie those whose courage knew no bounds,
amid the chaos, mud and nightmare sounds.

$\rightarrow$

Nameless ones, without a grave,
to mark a life they freely gave.
So I may live to see this day,
to watch the skylarks as they play,
hovering above my head,
guarding heroes in their bed,
of golden wheat and poppies red.

Background to *A SACRED PLACE*

I found myself reminiscing about the time spent as a child at Great Bavington, Northumberland at the beginning of WW2 and for some reason the myriad of birds to be found there, including skylarks. Eventually I realised that I needed to write something, but at the same time had to admit that what I knew about skylarks would not have covered a postage stamp.

However, as so often happened, the initial thought led to another poem related to the war but one that was not focused totally on skylarks. At the time, a title for the poem eluded me.

Some months after completion of the poem we were due to visit friends in France and planned to visit the valley of the Somme on our return journey. The year 2012 saw the 80th anniversary of the official opening of the Thiepval Memorial, which honours the 73,000 who died at the Battle of the Somme who have no known grave. It was also the 20th anniversary of the opening of the 'Historial de la Grande Guerre', an exhibition in the Citadel of Peronne, a town in one corner of the battlefield which had been the headquarters of the German forces.

From April to November there had been an extra exhibition telling the story of one of the 'missing' for each of the 141 days of the battle, supplemented by personal objects as well as others which illustrated a general remembrance theme.

Pam and Ken Linge, who created this extra exhibition, remind us that, such was the nature of the Somme battles, bodies could not be recovered while the fighting continued. Ceaseless pounding by artillery meant many of the dead went missing and were never recovered and explains why so many, after reburial, have the epitaph, "A soldier of the Great War known unto God."

Pam and Ken felt the need to have something more said about those whose names are written on the Thiepval Memorial to remind visitors that they were men who were loved and who loved in return. Their deaths left many families and friends to mourn for years to come and had a huge impact on the social structure. Using many fields of research, including an appeal for personal mementos and letters kept by families of some of these men who died, Pam and Ken were able to show a little of the personal background of individuals who would otherwise have remained just names amongst thousands of others. I believe this has become their life's work.

Surveying the once devastated landscape in WW1, now restored to farmland and sleepy villages and beautifully kept graves, I marvelled that man and nature had restored it to something so calm and beautiful and therefore worthy of being considered as a sacred place, inspiring the title I decided to give to my poem.

Recommended reading: *Missing of the Somme* by Ken and Pam Linge.

THE VOICE OF AN UNKNOWN SOLDIER

You walked past my grave this morning,
searching each row that was there.
Your lips were moving yet silent,
as you studied each name with care.

Who were you seeking dear lady,
was it Samson or Matty or me?
Young Pete's over there with his best pal Jim,
side by side neath the limb of a tree.

No one has stood at my graveside to weep,
nor laid a wreath at my feet.
But that doesn't really bother me much,
as this plot which is mine is kept neat.

No name adorns my headstone,
nor the age I had reached when I died.
My identity disc remained on a beach,
to be washed by a blood red tide.

Now there's nothing but dust neath this ground where you
trod,
for my spirit has long been free.
I'm one of the thousands known unto God
and He takes care of me.

Background to *THE VOICE OF AN UNKNOWN SOLDIER*

This poem proved to be the first of several poems depicting my thoughts at the time of various anniversaries of important moments during the two world wars.

It was written after an emotional last day of a tour of the D-Day landing sites and I had no idea that there would be more poems to follow.

We had encouraged our friend, Doreen Dew, to accompany us as she longed to revisit the grave of her brother Kenneth Terry, who was killed shortly after landing on D-Day and is buried at Bayeux in Normandy.

Doreen had enlisted in the Wrens during WW2 and was stationed on the Isle of Wight, working in Signals at the time of D-Day. She agreed that they knew "something big" was in the offing but had no real awareness of its significance. However, opening her bedroom curtains one morning, she found the entire sea stretching as far as Portsmouth covered in boats of every shape and size. Later Doreen was to realise that at some point her brother must have boarded one of these craft before leaving for France.

On the last day of our tour, Doreen laid a wreath on her brother's grave, which was a very touching moment for us all. Difficult for her though it was, she bravely recalled how she and her mother learned that her brother and his commanding officer were travelling to battalion headquarters when a

British vehicle travelling from the opposite direction struck a mine, killing the occupants of both vehicles. Had the orders for his company to leave the area not been changed, her brother would not have been on the road at the time.

Doreen at her brother's grave at Bayeaux.

Ken and his commanding officer are buried side by side, not far from a tree; a lovely way to acknowledge that, having died together, they were not to be divided in death. Later, as we headed towards our coach, it began to rain and, even though I was cold and tired, I could not help but notice the number of headstones inscribed with the words "An unknown soldier" or "Known unto God." By the time I reached the coach I was feeling very emotional, but did my best to hide my tears.

Once on the move I closed my eyes and then, to my astonishment, I clearly heard a man's voice in my head telling me that I had walked past his grave that morning and then essentially gave me the words of the poem line by line.

I realise this may be difficult for many to accept, nevertheless it is the truth. My writing materials were on the rack above so I could only repeat the lines I heard over and over again until we reached home and I could write down what I remembered.

Some months later, having polished the poem, my husband was desperate to have something fresh to include in the parish magazine he was editing at the time, close to Remembrance Sunday, so I left the poem on his desk. The next few moments were emotional ones for us both, as he had no idea I had written it and he was extremely moved by the words.

Later I was to realise that so many things I had witnessed on the tour were reflected in the poem. Apparently, so great was the carnage on Omaha beach where the Americans landed, that the sea actually turned red.

REFLECTIONS BEFORE INVASION
JUNE 4TH 1944 AND LATER

They stood in line along the pier,
shoulders stooped with battle gear.
No cheering crowds, no marching bands,
no outstretched arms to shake their hands.
Young men, one time with rosy cheeks,
who scrumped for apples and swam in creeks.
Stood forlorn in dawn's grey light,
while seagulls swooped in early flight.

What were their thoughts on that June day,
while boarding ships to sail away,
across a sea with rising swell,
leaving a land they knew so well?
Heading for shores where unknown foes,
more battle hardened, than many of those
we sent to stem the tide of war,
were watching on that fatal shore.

They stood in line across the pier,
shoulders stooped from passing year.
No cheering crowds, no marching bands,
no outstretched arms to shake their hands.
Old men, one time with rosy cheeks,
who scrumped for apples and swam in creeks
stood, just three, neath sunny skies,
while seagulls shrieked their strident cries.

→

What were their thoughts on that June day,
now seventy years had rolled away?
One wiped a tear from rheumy eye,
another coughed and gave a sigh.
their thoughts no doubt would have in mind,
the many pals they left behind,
the horrors seen, the scars they bear,
too grim to even want to share.

With final glance across the bay,
they turned as one to walk away.
Perhaps recalling rising swell,
while leaving a land they knew so well,
heading for shores where unknown foes,
more battle hardened than many of those,
we asked to stem the tide of war,
were dug in on that fatal shore.

But very soon, there'll be no more,
who witnessed carnage on that shore.
They've earned their time for rest and peace,
with other heroes long deceased,
never shirking a given task.
Remember us is all they ask.

Reflections.

Background to *REFLECTIONS BEFORE INVASION JUNE 4ᵀᴴ 1944 AND LATER*

We were holidaying in Devon at the time of the seventieth anniversary of D-Day, enjoying a day at Salcombe, one of the many places along that particular part of south Devon from which both British and American troops set sail for France on June 4th, 1944.

There were several television programmes during the week related to the anniversary and a full day's coverage of remembrance services taking place at Calais. Sitting on a small viewing area of the harbour, we were able to read the monument dedicated to the American troops who left there that day.

The memorial at Salcombe.

I had recently been reading a book entitled *Tommy at War*, learning of the men who volunteered from northern towns and villages in the UK at the beginning of 1914 and noting the send-off they received. Schools were closed and there was much flag waving, brass bands marching ahead of them and people eager to shake them by the hands as they left for war.

However, in 1944 the largest armada ever assembled, consisting of nearly seven thousand ships of all sizes, stood off the coast of Normandy as dawn broke on June 6th. Preparations for this started as early as 1941 but such was the secrecy that it was known to very few. As a result, 100,000 fighting men left our shores to begin one of the epic assaults in history without a good luck or God bless.

In the order of the day issued by General D. Eisenhower, Commander-in-Chief were included the following words, *"Your task will not be an easy one. Your enemy is well trained, well equipped and battle hardened. He will fight hard and savagely."*

Franklin D. Roosevelt, president of the USA, in a broadcast to his nation said, *"This is a struggle to preserve our republic, our religion and our civilisation and to set free a suffering humanity."*

Meanwhile, Field Marshal Erwin Rommel, Commandant of German Army Group B, had this to say, *"If we do not succeed in our mission to close the seas to the allies or in, the first forty-*

eight hours, to throw them back, their invasion will be successful."

These stirring words, from three recognised leaders at the time, are a fitting reminder of what those taking part were facing.

None of us can even begin to imagine the thoughts of the men themselves, so I have tried to imagine the scene on the day itself and then to compare it, some seventy years later, as three veterans make a private, personal, visit to the scene of their departure.

THE FIRST DAY OF THE BATTLE OF THE SOMME
JULY 1ST 1916.

Do poppies still grow on that sacred ground,
their tall stems crowned in red.
And is the skylark's joyful sound,
a tribute to honour the dead?

For there one hundred years ago,
brave men left safety at walking pace.
Believing their battle-hardened foe,
had perished beneath the earth's dark face.

For had not their guns for seven days,
pounded the earth both day and night?
While men from both sides were mentally crazed,
by remorseless noise to add to their plight.

They steadily walked across no-man's land,
still unchallenged by enemy shell,
until those in the lead could see first hand,
the undamaged barbed wire, before they fell.

Those further back knew a moment of fear,
as endless shells poured down like rain
while machine gun bullets ended life of those near,
as the air was rent by screams of pain.

No retreat the order made clear,
as those still to come had nowhere to hide.
They could only move forward 'mid chaos and fear,
as they trembled, stumbled together and died.

$\rightarrow$

As silence descended at roll call that night,
when name after name brought no replies,
even some officers try as they might,
failed to stop tears from clouding their eyes.

Thousands were slaughtered on that day alone,
young men who answered the call to fight,
to stand against foe, who threatened their home,
no longer knew dawn, just endless night.

No poppies now grow on that sacred ground,
for farming has banished them all.
But now and again it's as if there's a sound,
akin to a skylark's call.

As if a thousand voices speak
from beneath that nurtured earth,
begging us all not to be weak,
but to fight for freedom's worth.

Thiepval
Monument.

Background to *THE FIRST DAY OF THE BATTLE OF THE SOMME JULY 1ST 1916*

It has been suggested that I chose a difficult subject when I wrote this poem. However, in my defence, it chose me.

I have read extensively about this battle and have my own thoughts about the decisions made by the generals. However, it is always easy for those not there at the time and with better communication than in 1914 and more knowledge of modern warfare, to stand in justice.

So something compelled me to write my thoughts about what some troops might have experienced on the first day of the battle. With so many who went over the top that day, there must have been a varied response from the enemy, depending on the positions of the regiments involved along a very wide front. I have read that one northern regiment opposite a German position with little defence, because it was not thought to be in a vulnerable position, walked over with ease and captured several prisoners with little loss to themselves.

It is mind numbing learning the number of men slaughtered on that first day alone. Not to make some attempt to acknowledge the sheer waste of humanity in this personal tribute and the effect it had for years to come, would be a travesty.

During a television programme relating to the one hundredth anniversary of the battle, historians were quoting from both British and German accounts.

One German officer had written that the continuous bombardment almost drove them crazy and prevented rations reaching them. However, he claimed that the worst moment came when the bombardment ceased, indicating an attack was imminent. However, to their surprise the attacking troops walked forward instead of charging, which allowed them time to move to the forward trenches and man the guns. He reckoned that had they charged the outcome would have been somewhat different.

THE LAST FEW HOURS

Despatches recorded a quiet night,
as dawn's grey fingers promised light.
Little movement in the enemy trench,
just the constant reeking stench,
from putrid mud and bloody gore,
which found its way into every pore.

Morale was low in every sense,
as moving like robots men checked their defence.
Still alert for an incoming shell,
which could herald the start of a day from hell.
Nevertheless a watch must be kept,
so they took it in turns, while others slept.

Nothing stirred outside on the pockmarked ground,
where thousands were wounded or died without sound.
No incoming shells to plough up the earth,
which season by season had witnessed the birth,
of fresh grass and flowers and ripe golden grain.
Nurtured by sunshine and soft summer rain.

With faces grey and nerves stretched tight,
their bodies poised for fight or flight.
They fought their own demons as best they could,
longing for sleep and nourishing food.
Then the sound of action and a cry that was new,
from an eagle-eyed sentry, had them all standing to.

$\rightarrow$

With trembling fingers and lump in his throat,
the sergeant accepted the runner's note.
Searched for his orders, then read them again,
while turning still trembling, to share with his men,
the order which stated the Germans seek peace.
They've agreed to surrender, all firing to cease.

In weeks which would follow as word spread worldwide,
they would dance in the streets and thank God they'd
survived.
But there in that trench, where a vigil they'd kept,
grown men sank to their knees in the mud
and just wept.

Weariness
© Daniel Foucart

Background to *THE LAST FEW HOURS*

On yet another anniversary of the ending of WW2 there were TV programmes about the various celebrations that had taken place throughout the country when the war ended. However, they did focus on central London, with The Royal Family appearing on the balcony at the palace, with Sir Winston Churchill, although there were some pictures of the street parties as well.

I was fortunate to be in London at that time as my father had some leave but was required to return to India for a while, so we were visiting Sid and Mary Bagshaw, friends of my parents.

Later I was to learn that Sid Bagshaw had first met my father in 1915 when, as a very new young soldier in WW1, he attended a church service in London and was befriended by Sid after the service and invited back for lunch. The friendship remained very close until Sid's death.

There are several reminders of that particular London visit which are very special to me. Essentially, on the train journey to London we shared a compartment with the Dowager Duchess of Northumberland, whom my father recognised although the other travellers did not. There were no first and second class carriages during the war years but my father had heard the porter address her as Your Grace and to ask her if this carriage would be satisfactory, She was charming and insisted on sharing her sandwiches with us all and taught me and another child how to play Battleships.

My father was determined to show me the main sights of London, so I had his total company for one whole day having seen very little of him for six years. Later he booked seats for a production of *Yeoman of the Guard*. I had only once been to the theatre, to see *Peter Pan*, so this was a very exciting evening for me and I was spellbound by the music and singing and it was probably the start of my love of light operatic shows.

However, watching the celebrations again on TV, I realised that I had never witnessed any programme, nor reports about the effect of the ceasefire on the troops, some of whom were still fighting. I felt compelled to try to imagine the impact it may have had on the men at the time.

My husband remarked that I had instinctively gone back to WW1 and back into the trenches. However, for me war is war, no matter where it took place or ended and I felt that the impact on the men must have been very similar, no matter where or when they were fighting or imprisoned, but these are entirely my thoughts and my only deep regret is for those who, for whatever reason, were forced to keep fighting by their superior officers, resulting in more than one being killed after the official announcement to cease firing.

THE ROAD TO THE MENIN GATE

I thought I saw some soldiers,
march down the Menin Road,
swinging arms and heads held high,
in spite of heavy load.

I longed to halt their journey,
for somehow knew their fate,
having seen the many names,
above the Menin Gate.

They heeded not my call to stop
and then I realised why.
They were the ghosts of many men,
who passed this way to die.

They could not see me standing there,
for I was not yet born,
when they and others walked this road,
to die before next dawn.

Standing by the Menin Road,
I felt their ghosts pass by,
now knowing destiny ordained,
the place where they would die.

THE MEMORIAL WALL

So many names on a memorial wall, skilfully carved with care,
one perhaps a relation of one of us standing there.
So many names on a memorial wall, too many to read every one,
yet each left friends and relations to mourn for years to come.
So many names on a memorial wall, skilfully carved with pride,
once were loving human beings who risked their lives and died.
All those names on a memorial wall, but who in years to come
will honour endless lists of men who fought for freedom and won?

2018 Memorial Service at Menin Gate.

Background to THE MENIN GATE and
THE MEMORIAL WALL

In all honesty I cannot recall what triggered off these two poems although they were written on the same day. During this time I was reading a lot of personal accounts about the war and something triggered a memory of my visit to Ypres and the ceremony at 8pm each evening.

My husband and I had been given the honour of laying a wreath on behalf of our group, as a tribute to the Essex soldiers. Instructions from those in charge of the ceremony were brief. However, we had to walk together up the steps carrying the wreath. On reaching the top we had to bow and take one step forward to place the wreath before taking a step back. After bowing once more we had to separate and descend the steps separately, one at each side.

Sea Cadets lined the steps either side and for me this was the most nerve-wracking moment because it was not long after a bilateral knee operation so I depended a lot on a stick for support. However, needs must and thankfully as the steps were wide I managed to keep pace with my husband to arrive safely at the road. Just before the last step two of our group held up their hands to give us a mark of ten out of ten to indicate well done. A treasured moment.

I think it was the association of names on the Menin Gate and on some of the memorials we had seen that probably prompted writing the two poems almost together.

It is hard to accept the hundreds of names of those killed, simply by seeing the names on a memorial. For me it was the hundreds of headstones in the cemeteries which made the biggest impact and awareness of the huge loss of life. One could spend a lifetime standing in front of each headstone to acknowledge and give thanks to each individual and still never finish.

I have very little awareness of the Boer War so don't really think about it, although there were men who fought in it as well as in WW1. So how long, I wonder, will the current generation give the two world wars a thought once my peers have died? I cannot but wonder what will happen to these memorials in years to come and whether anybody will care.

We owe a great deal to the French and Belgian people, who set aside so much land and continue to respect and care for the cemeteries.

PROGRESS

Think back to a time when there were no drains,
rubbish and filth lay rotting in streets.
People died young from their aches and pains,
while some children lacked shoes for their frozen feet.

Think back to a time when there were no trains,
transport relied upon horses and carts.
Ships were dependent on wind for their sails
and no aeroplanes flew to foreign parts.

Think back to a time when houses were dark,
candles were used for light.
While many could only leave their mark,
deprived of schooling and learning to write.

Think back to a time when deep underground,
men crouched to hew coal in the dark.
Their lungs thick with dust as they feared for the sound
of explosive gas from a possible spark.

Think back to a time without phones and TV,
when letters were written by hand
and if anyone called we offered them tea,
then spoke of the weather and things we had planned.

We've come a long way with science and skills,
sent men to the moon who walked in space.
Conquered diseases, found relief for most ills,
yet still there remains so much hatred with race.

$\rightarrow$

The progress we made with material things,
makes life easier we cannot deny.
Yet poverty remains with all that it brings
and weapons and drugs now cause youngsters to die.

Too many leave school without any skills,
books remain unread,
while we litter our streets with rubbish still,
and graffiti soils buildings instead.

We're rushing like lemmings for all we can get,
so fast we cannot keep pace.
Some churches stand empty and wars threaten yet,
for there's still so much hatred with race.

Background to PROGRESS

It would be interesting to know what my father and Lucienne's would have made of the state of the world today. In fact what would all of those who fought in world wars, or who were made homeless or lost loved ones think of it all?

Doubtless they would marvel at the achievements in science and commerce. But what of relationships between nations? Just how much have we learned from the past? Are we in danger of repeating some of the mistakes as greed and the wish to dominate by some, continue to rear their heads, while we sit back until it is too late and we find history repeating itself?

Harry Boyce, a Canadian veteran of the Great War, was 103 when he addressed this message to future generations:

LEST WE FORGET.

"Maintain peace. Nothing can be gained by warfare. Settle disagreements rather than go to war over them because one war brings on another…"

WHITE UPRIGHT STONES

There is a place where I have been where lie at rest so
many men,
marked by white, upright stones that mock the innocence
of those,
lulled by adventure to far away shores, never to return to
childhood haunts.

Passing seasons tell their tale.

First Spring, which cradled new-born seeds
and nourished them to full-blown stance, while mothers
watched with daily pride,
each faltering step to manly stride.

Hot summer suns brought strength to limbs, and filled their
heads with fearless thoughts, so nothing daunted manly pride
when called to arms as thousands died.

But Autumn came with drenching rain, to numb their limbs to
leaden walk
and turned the once hard, solid ground, to treacherous mud,
where fallen failed to rise again and begged a bullet through
their brain.

Then Winter, with her fingers white, filled the ground with
many shrouds
for those young men, who learned too late, that war was not a
childhood game, just one large grave for endless slain.

This was the place which I have seen and wept beside those upright stones,
that mark the life of those brave men who, had they lived to tell their tale, would speak of hell called Passchendaele.

Troops at Passchendaele.

Background to WHITE UPRIGHT STONES

My friend Chania's experience at Ypres, where she acted as a guide at the Tyne Cot Cemetery and also at the Menin Gate Ceremony in 2018, had left a great impression on her. Later, having visited Australia and New Zealand, she wrote to say how privileged she felt seeing the homeland of so many of the men she left behind in Ypres, who failed to return to their childhood home.

The author Will Fowler in his book *Ypres 1914-15: A Battle Story* refers to the memorials at The Menin Gate and Tyne Cot and the overwhelming number of names recorded of British and Commonwealth soldiers, who were killed in the Ypres Salient during the First World War, but have no known grave. He also refers to the numerous individual cemeteries at what were possibly the sites of field dressing and casualty stations.

These graves were not in rows, but dotted here and there where the men were buried, often moments after they died, when there was a lull in the fighting. Such was the carnage, some headstones bear the words 'buried somewhere in this cemetery'. Names were recorded, but the bodies were lost in the mud, destroyed by repeated artillery fire.

Working in one of these casualty stations was a Canadian Army Surgeon, Lieutenant Colonel John McCrae MD. From the papers of Edward W.B. Morrison we read that their headquarters were on top of the bank of the Ypres Canal and

John McCrae had his dressing station dug in a hole at the bottom of the bank.

It was during this time that he wrote his poem *In Flanders Fields*, describing the crosses "row on row" which marked the graves and the poppies which blow.

It is difficult, to say the least, to even begin to imagine the conditions that the combination of the heaviest rain in 30 years and constant shelling did to the ground on which the soldiers fought. Thick glutinous mud, which trapped man, beast and equipment.

Harry Patch, the last surviving soldier of the Great War, served at Passchendaele at the age of nineteen. Badly wounded by shrapnel, he never got over his three mates dying beside him, as they were heading from the front line to a resting area. I personally will always remember the tears he fought during a television interview, where he spoke of having shared everything with his three mates until then; he felt "he should have gone with them". He was 111 years of age when he died in 2009.

Tyne Cot

CONCLUSION

Since completing the anthology I have been fortunate to be able to return to the battlefields and share memorable moments with others from the Commonwealth, most of whom laid wreaths for family members, or their individual country.

Heading for Portsmouth before an overnight sailing to Ouistreham, for Caen, we visited Southwick House where we learned some of the details of Operations Overlord and Neptune and stood in the room where General Eisenhower, after considerable discussions with his advisers, uttered the words, "Let's go," to start the D-Day invasion. I cannot deny there was a lump in my throat acknowledging the courage and bravery and risk of that individual decision to which history would hold him to account.

Our first breakfast on French soil was taken at Café Gondrée, the first house to be liberated on D-Day and a great favourite with veterans of that day when visiting the area at Pegasus Bridge. The family had given valuable intelligence to the Allied forces before the landing and the café is now run by the daughter of the family who was a child at the time of the liberation.

With the blessing of my friend Doreen Dew, who was no longer able to travel that distance, I laid a wreath on her brother's grave at Bayeux Commonwealth War Graves Commission Cemetery in Normandy. We were able to contact

Doreen from the graveside as the wreath was laid, so she was present in spirit at the special moment.

Another memorable occasion occurred at the American Cemetery when, having laid their wreath, the wife of an American couple sang their national anthem. It was as if even the birds stopped singing while so many stood silent until she had finished.

A young guide called Chania Fox at Tyne Cot Cemetery, the largest Commonwealth War Graves Commission Cemetery where 11,000 graves stand, was introduced to me after telling our tour guide that she was especially interested in war poetry. Eventually she asked me if I would recite one of my poems, and I chose *The Memorial Wall*.

What was gratifying was her awareness of what she and her colleagues were learning through their work at the site. Commenting on how much they had gained from talking to many visitors, they had agreed that it was now up to them to carry the torch to the next generation, so people continued to learn of the travesty of world wars and the need to recognise that nothing is gained, other than further destruction and loss of life. I am delighted that Chania continues to correspond with me and am grateful for the photograph of The Menin Gate ceremony she sent on Remembrance Sunday 2018 where she was helping.

In recent correspondence from her tour of New Zealand and Australia, Chania acknowledges how fortunate she has been to visit the homeland where so many she left behind in cemeteries in Ypres, were never able to return.

In November 2014 a new memorial unknown to me, called The Ring Of Memory, was opened by President Hollande. An oval-shaped enclosure with panels listing, strictly in alphabetical order, without nationality, 580,000 names of all forty nationalities who died in the Nord/Pas-de-Calais region in 1914-18. 290,000 are British Empire. It is of outstanding quality and highly recommended to visit.

It would take another book to cover all of the very memorable moments encountered on the tour, but it would be remiss of me not to mention the second opportunity the tour gave me to visit The Last Post Ceremony at the Menin Gate. Depending on the numbers of daily visitors, who come from all over the world to lay wreaths and acknowledge the names of the fallen, the ceremony can last a variable length of time. Nevertheless, although my husband and I were not taking part as before, it remained a very moving occasion which continues every evening at 8pm to remember the sacrifice of those in WW1, known as The Great War.

I have a great love of my country and the county of Northumberland where I was born and just wish that more emphasis was focussed on our past achievements in areas of science and commerce. Having produced so many men and women of influence, why are we so apparently reluctant to broadcast them and to hand down our pride to our children both at home and in schools? Children should be encouraged to have more respect and knowledge of the history of this great country of ours for which so many gave their lives in time of need.

ABOUT THE AUTHOR

Anne was born and raised in Northumberland and educated at Whitley Bay Grammar School before commencing training as a nurse at Newcastle General Hospital, qualifying in 1956.

Married with two children and five grandchildren she had to move house on several occasions, due to her husband's work, but has resided in Epping, Essex for many years.

Her interests include singing in choirs and amateur operatic societies, following some voice training, until severe hearing loss curtailed performances. An avid reader with a keen interest in the history of warfare, she has toured many battlefields in France and Belgium and treasures her friendship with Lucienne Lerch, in Alsace. A friendship which arose during a school exchange when they were sixteen, encouraged by their respective fathers, who each served and survived both world wars.

Now retired she works with the Pastoral Care Team at St. Michael's Church, Theydon Mount, with Stapleford Tawney.

She started writing poetry following a very emotional encounter during a battlefield tour of the D-Day landing sites, which led to this collection of poems.

GIVE THANKS THIS DAY

Take time each day at setting sun,
to look upon a day now gone.
Thank God for having had this day,
to toil at tasks which came your way.

Don't dwell on things as yet undone,
just gaze at length at setting sun
and think of those who long ago,
left our shores to battle foe.

So few returned to live a day,
that you enjoyed in some small way.
So count your blessings one by one,
as your day ends at setting sun.

PRINTED AND BOUND BY:

Copytech (UK) Limited trading as Printondemand-worldwide,
9 Culley Court, Bakewell Road, Orton Southgate.
Peterborough, PE2 6XD, United Kingdom.